Bankruptcy – Your Personal Finances are a Mess, so You Think it's the Only Answer. Maybe. Maybe Not!

What you should know BEFORE you file.

I0463227

Judy Wesener

ISBN-13:
978-1463751333

ISBN-10:
1463751338

"Forgive yourself for your faults and your mistakes and move on." -Les Brown

.

TABLE OF CONTENTS

Introduction

Does it ever feel like there is no way out? Are your bills so far behind that you keep waiting for the repo man to come knocking on the door? Expecting him to come for the car, the house and the furniture? Every time the phone rings, do you feel sick, knowing it's yet another bill collector?

If you think bankruptcy is the only answer, you really need to read this book first. It wasn't written to be all-inclusive. It's not going to give your every single piece of information as to the ins and outs of bankruptcy. However, it will provide you with the basic knowledge you need to precede in an informed manner. Also, you may find there just may be a few things you could do to possibly avoid taking such drastic action.

This book presents simple to understand, basic information. It's meant to help you to decide what actions you'll need to take next. When people find themselves in a desperate financial situation, they simply don't have any idea what to do next. Many times, the lack of knowledge, stress of debt and fears for their future, will cause them to take no action at all. By taking no action, things will only continue to get worse. You have to take some type of action. Hopefully this book will give you an idea on what action you'll need to take, to get you headed in a positive direction.

There are a few options you should explore first, before filing for bankruptcy. If you find none of these options work for you, then there are certain steps you should take BEFORE you actually file your bankruptcy paperwork.

One thing you don't want to do is pretend it'll all go away. It won't. This is one problem that only gets worse with time. When your finances start falling apart, address the issues head-on. The longer you wait, the more everything will unravel and the harder it'll be to work with your debtors.

If you find, that after looking at all your options, bankruptcy is your only choice, then make sure you do everything correctly BEFORE you file. There are some very important actions you need to take, or not to take, to make your bankruptcy go as smoothly as possible.

Take it from someone who's been there. One bad business deal caused my financial life to spin out of control and it all happened in less than 6 months! It happened so fast; I didn't even know what to do next. I didn't know my options.

Believe me, I made way too many mistakes! I hung on much to long to a sinking ship. I tried frantically to pay all the bills that just kept rolling in every month. Even empting my considerable saving account and taking a huge chuck of money out of my IRA couldn't save me. I had done these things in a desperate attempt NOT to file for bankruptcy.

In the end, after everything I had tried to do, it was all for nothing, because I still had to file for a chapter 7 bankruptcy. So now, not only was my present affected, my future was as well. Now I really found myself in dire straights, because I had also affected my future by withdrawing nearly all my IRA. This was a huge mistake!

I'm writing this in hopes of giving someone else enough information, so they can avoid the same pitfalls I encountered. I found myself trying to survive not only the enormous stress of my financial current situation, but also the uncertainty of what my future would hold, now that all my retirement money was gone.

If nothing else, you'll know what questions to ask. Don't you hate it when someone asks if you have any questions and you don't even know enough to be able to form a question? You just sit there and stare blankly, thinking to yourself; 'I can't ask a question because I don't even know what to ask!'

I know it can be like being caught in a nightmare. It may seem that there's no way out. Just remember, you do have options. The most important thing you need to remember is to "get all your ducks into a row".

Preparation is key, not only for your present situation, but also for your future.

Misconceptions Pertaining to Bankruptcy

In today's world, the overall economy is just so unpredictable; even a few simple financial mistakes can result in economic ruin. As a result, a sharp rise has been seen in the number of bankruptcy cases being filed everyday.

Bankruptcy has always been a last resort for financially troubled people. Most people are not aware of the actual process and it's long-term effects on their lives. This book was written in hopes to remove the most common misconceptions regarding bankruptcy, from your mind.

Will you lose your job if you file for bankruptcy? There's no legal precedent to imply that an employer can fire you just because you have filed for bankruptcy. Your employer must have a legal and documented cause to fire you. Just bare in mind, that if you become so preoccupied with your bankruptcy that you're no longer performing your job duties, you're employer will have just cause to terminate you. There are rare cases where you may have been required to sign a document stating, as a term of employment, that you would maintain a good credit score and never file for bankruptcy. If this is the case, then you would have broken the contract to stay financially sound, and your employer can make the decision to terminate you.

A rather absurd concept is that just saying the words "I am declaring a bankruptcy" in public clears all the debts of a person. In reality, bankruptcy is a lengthy process, taking somewhere around six months, or longer, to complete and leaving a strong impression on your whole life. For some people it can take as long as ten years to get back a good credit rating.

Yes, you can file the bankruptcy paperwork yourself, but there's can be a large volume of paperwork to file. The bankruptcy laws are complex, and so many complications can arise. For this reason, most people will hire a professional, such as a bankruptcy attorney, instead of filing the bankruptcy documents by themselves.

Some people fear filing for bankruptcy because they think their financial situation may get worse in the future. They believe they won't be able to do anything because they would have already used their bankruptcy option. It is possible to file for bankruptcy several times during your lifetime. Naturally there are some restrictions in place to prevent abuse.

Technically you can file for bankruptcy as often as you like, but you probably won't get the results you want.

Put simply, in most states, if you've had a chapter 7 bankruptcy discharged, then you can't file for another chapter 7 for at least 8 years or 6 years from a prior chapter 13 filing.

A chapter 13 can be filed 4 years from a prior chapter 7 filing or 2 years from a prior 13 filing. These time periods are measured from the commencement date of the case, not the discharge date. Remember, the bankruptcy laws are subject to change, so always double check these numbers.

One thing that you need to remember is that if one spouse files and the other one doesn't, the one who didn't file could find themselves responsible for the debts. You'll need to review this very carefully before filing. This is where you really need to seek the advice of a bankruptcy lawyer before taking any action.

Personal Bankruptcy

Bankruptcy should never be taken lightly. It's a major, life changing decision.

If you find yourself seriously considering filing for bankruptcy, you've probably had a major "life event" occur. This event could be a job loss, major illness, divorce, loss of income, a failed business or you may have found yourself overwhelmed and overextended.

People today are finding themselves in a financial dilemma more often then ever before in history and unfortunately, these numbers are continuing to rise.

The main purpose of bankruptcy is to give honest debtors a fresh start. This is done by clearing most debts and discharging debtors from legal obligations for those debts. The courts are provided with non-exempt assets, which they may, or may not, distributed among your creditors.

A bankruptcy case is started with the filing of a petition. This petition declares the debtors financial information and states their intent to declare bankruptcy.

The most common filing is for a Chapter 7 bankruptcy, which is a liquidation of assets. This is where the debtor's non-exempt assets are sold off and distributed on the basis of priority amongst the creditors. However, there are some assets that are exempt.

A Chapter 13 bankruptcy is also available to individuals. Chapter 13 allows a debtor to keep property and pay debts over time, usually three to five years.

In 2005, the US Bankruptcy Laws were changed. There are now more restrictions for filing both a chapter 7 and chapter 13 bankruptcy. Before the 2005 revision, filers could choose which code they wanted to file under. Income didn't matter, however, that has all changed since 2005, and now income is a larger consideration.

One of the biggest changes applies to those with a higher income, they may be required to file under a chapter 13 and therefore pay off some of their incurred debt. In addition to the new income demands, all disposable income left, after paying actual living expenses, must now go into their repayment plan.

The IRS will now determine the allowed living expenses, not the actual living expenses, if their income is higher than the median income in their state.

Additionally, there's now mandatory credit and financial counseling debtors must complete before and after filing for chapter 7 bankruptcy. The counseling is designed to keep people aware of their spending and keep them on track.

At the end of the counseling, you'll be presented with a certificate that you will need to give to the bankruptcy trustee.

- Pre-filing, individuals must complete credit counseling

- Post-filing, they must complete financial budgeting

Although the majority of this counseling provides information most people already have. I, personally, did pick up some interesting suggestions, so it wasn't really a total waste of time and money (yes, you have to pay to attend).

Alternatives to Bankruptcy

Many people, who find themselves in financial trouble, immediately turn to bankruptcy for relief. This decision should be considered as a last resort, not your first course of action. You do have other options you can explore before taking such drastic action.

Talk to Your Creditors

First and foremost, talk with your creditors and try to work something out with them. You'll find that many of them will try to work with you on a repayment plan. Unfortunately, some will not be willing to negotiate with you, but don't let that discourage you from trying.

Just pick up the phone, make the call and see what you can do. You'd be surprised how understanding some of them can be and how ready they are to help you come up with a possible solution.

Also, don't just give up because the first person you spoke to said, "No". Call again and ask to speak with a supervisor/manager/owner. The first person you spoke with may not have had the authority to offer you any type of solution.

Be sure you explain your circumstances to them. Tell them you're considering filing bankruptcy, but you want to try to work something out first. Be as straightforward and concise as possible, they need to understand this is a serious situation.

Take a Long, Hard Look at Your Finances

Get organized and actually write out a budget. This doesn't need to be anything fancy. Just start with your monthly income, and then deduct your monthly household expenses.

Now take a look at where your money is being spent. How can you cutback? All of us have areas we could actually cut back a little and save some money. Every little bit helps.

You could also cut way back and live very simply for a number of years. This method is much easier if there's just you or even one other person. However, it's very difficult to cut back drastically if you have children.

Maybe you could start buying groceries in bulk, or only buy items when they're on sale. Start using coupons. Many libraries have an area where people drop off the coupons they aren't going to use. Also, you can print out coupons, for all types of items, online. Gather the Sunday Newspaper (or whichever day your local paper puts in the coupons) from family, friends and neighbors. Cut out the coupons you'll need and use them.

Maybe you could cut back a little on your telephone, cell phone, or TV services. Remember, this isn't going to be forever, just until you can get back on your feet.

Next take a good look at your credit cards. Can you move the balance from a high interest card to one with lower interest? It's very important to get rid of the high interest cards altogether. High interest credit cards are a money pit; you'll never get ahead with any of them. Be sure to call your credit card companies and try to negotiate for lower interest rates. Again, don't give up after the first attempt. Call back in a day or so, to see if maybe the next person will be willing to work with you to lower your interest rate.

Is there any chance you can refinance your mortgage or vehicle loans? If you can bring the payments down on these items, it'll give you a little extra money to put towards your other bills.

Debt Consolidation

After you've done everything you can, it might be wise to speak with a non-profit debt consolidator. Many people who think they're in deep financial trouble may actually only be in borderline difficulty. With some help and creative financial dealings, debts can many times be paid off without the initiating of a bankruptcy case.

Be careful when choosing a debt consolidator. Do your research. Watch out for scammers. Unfortunately there are a lot of people out there who are ready to pounce on someone who is desperate and already in a bad situation. You can avoid them simply by doing your homework in advance.

Bankruptcy Lawyer

OK, so you've tried your very best but everything has failed, now it's time to start thinking about consulting a bankruptcy attorney.

However, before you do contact anyone or file any paperwork yourself, you need to be sure that you've followed the suggestions in this book. There are some actions you need to take BEFORE you file. The following chapters of this book will provide you with suggestions on what you need to do or what actions not to take, before filing. There are some actions you may be considering that will actually cause you problems later on, or even slow the whole process down.

When you have everything in order and you're ready to proceed, you'll want to talk with a bankruptcy lawyer. These lawyers specialize in the entire bankruptcy process. They'll explain everything from filing the paperwork, to how to deal with creditor calls, as well as the meeting of creditors and how the court hearing process will work.

Most bankruptcy attorneys offer a free consultation. Be sure to take advantage of this option, before you make any decisions as to which attorney you want to handle this process for you. I personally interviewed three lawyers before I choose the one I wanted to use to help me.

Not all bankruptcy lawyers are trustworthy. So again, do your research. Talk to your family and friends to see if they have any attorney's they know or have used. Do an Internet search on the lawyer you're considering. Make sure there isn't a bunch of negative information out there pertaining to this lawyer. If there is, look elsewhere. You don't need any more problems right now.

When you do file, keep in mind that false filing for bankruptcy is a crime and punishable in court. Be honest with all the information you provide.

.

Do You Meet the Requirements for Bankruptcy?

You'll need to check the requirements for bankruptcy in your state. Although many of the requirements are nationwide, each state is slightly different.

Generally, when your debt is too high and your income too low, you probably will not qualify for a chapter 13 bankruptcy. On the other hand, when your income is too high and your debts low, you probably will not qualify for a chapter 7 bankruptcy.

In some cases, you may not qualify for either. If you find this happens in your case, this is a sure sign that you may not have thought through your other options and need to go back and revisit all other options. You're one of the lucky ones who actually still have choices.

If you do qualify to file, be sure to consider all of your property and debts. What will happen to your home? Will you be able to keep your car? Is your retirement plan safe? Every state has different specification when to comes to these assets, so make sure that you understand how your property will be affected. Also, it's important to begin compiling lists of your assets and debts. Remember that some debts cannot be wiped out, like child support payments.

Once you have all your information compiled, you can begin the declaration process. It is best to work with a lawyer or financial professional to complete this task, and remember to always be completely honest. This is legal issue and anything less than the truth is considered fraud.

Declaring bankruptcy is not for everyone, but it can work for some people. In fact, for some, it may be their only option.

Bankruptcy in a Nut Shell

When you find yourself facing financial troubles, you're under enormous pressure to resolve them. You basically have four options:

1. Work with your creditors
2. Cut back your spending and get on a budget
3. Debt consolidation
4. Bankruptcy

When you file for bankruptcy it means that you have become legally insolvent. Bankruptcy can come in two types:

1. Most Common - Voluntary Bankruptcy- where you choose to file a petition with a claim that you

have no funds left and will not be able to repay your loans.

2. Uncommon - Involuntary Bankruptcy - is where lenders or creditors file the petition in the court against you.

The court essentially decides whether your claim can, in fact, be proven or not, on the basis of the details provided by you. If the court decides that you will not be able to repay your debt, they will discharge your bankruptcy.

Before you file for the bankruptcy, you must keep in mind that generally, you will face greater difficulty in getting any new loans, buying a car, finding some apartments or purchasing a house. Your credit score will have the record of your bankruptcy for a period of 10 years.

Now you'll be told that your slate has been "wiped clean", so you won't have any problems getting credit. Unfortunately, this isn't necessarily true. Before my financial troubles, I had a credit score in the 800's, but that doesn't matter once you file and your bankruptcy is discharged. I was able to get a credit card, at twice the going interest rate. When trying to purchase a new car, I found the same terms. I could get the car, but the interest rate was unreasonable. And many creditors weren't interested in extending credit to me under any conditions.

So I guess what that all means is that yes, you can get credit, but expect the interest rates to be considerably higher than what you may have experienced before the bankruptcy. Also, expect the lenders to be much more strict and the loans much harder to acquire. Don't be surprised when many lenders turn you down completely.

Handling Creditor Calls After Filing

As soon as the bankruptcy petition is stamped "Relief Ordered" upon filing, you're immediately protected from your creditors. Creditors are not allowed to call or harass you in any way. They're required by law to stop all collection efforts against you. This action is called an "automatic stay".

If a creditor does call you or attempt to collect on a debt, you should immediately notify the creditor, in writing, that you have filed for bankruptcy. You'll need to provide them with either the case number and filing date or a copy of the petition showing it was filed.

If you have an attorney, you simply refer them to your lawyer and the lawyer will handle providing all necessary information to the creditor.

If the creditor continues to attempt to contact you, you may be entitled to initiate legal action against them.

How Creditors are Notified of Your Bankruptcy Protection

When you file for bankruptcy protection, you will have provided a list of all your creditors, along with their addresses.

The bankruptcy court will notify everyone on that list, by mail. When they notify your creditors, they'll provide the following information:

- Tell them that you've filed for bankruptcy
- Give them the case number
- Advise them of the automatic stay
- Provide them with the name of the trustee assigned to the case
- Give them the deadline for filing any objections to the dismissal of the debts
- Where to file claims

This may vary slightly, depending on the type of bankruptcy filed.

This is the reason why it's very important to include everyone you owe money to when you fill out your paperwork. You want to be sure to include all creditors, don't leave anyone out. Go over your list several times, if necessary, to ensure accuracy.

Forgot to Add a Debt?

If you forgot to include a debt when you originally filed your paperwork, you can typically file an amendment to correct it. Keep in mind that you're submitting the petition under penalty of perjury, so be very careful with your initial filing.

Also, you need to realize that any debt you miss adding, won't be discharged and you will have to pay all money owed to that creditor.

So in other words, if you owe $10,000 on a credit card, and forget to include it in your filing, you will still owe that money. A discharge of a bankruptcy only covers the debts you've listed, if it's not listed, you'll still be responsible to pay the entire amount of the debt.

Dealing with a Bankruptcy Lawyer

There are several different kinds of bankruptcy, depending on whether it's a personal or business bankruptcy. It's very important to consult with a competent lawyer to discuss which type is right for you.

The most common bankruptcy filings are chapter 13 and chapter 7. The differences are dramatic. It's important for you to know what you're doing and which one makes the most sense in your situation. Knowing your exact financial state is very important. Don't guess, have a complete written record of all income and debt.

A qualified and competent bankruptcy lawyer can help you sort through all of the financial pro's and cons. They can recommend the best course of action to make sure you come out on top, once the whole state of affairs is over.

These are difficult times, and if you are contemplating bankruptcy, you need to make sure you find the right lawyer to represent you. One thing you should be careful is to find a reputable lawyer.

If you are unable to pay your lawyer all of his fees up front, offer to make payments and if you have to use some collateral for security, make sure that you specifically spell out the terms you and the lawyer have agreed upon. Also, very important, get everything in writing! Make sure it's very detailed and concise, with nothing left to interpretation.

Choosing Your Bankruptcy Lawyer

One of the most vital decisions you will need to contemplate is which bankruptcy attorney will be right for you. Picking a bankruptcy attorney out of the phone book may not be in your best interests. Filing bankruptcy requires solid legal advice, practical wisdom and common sense.

When you set up your appointment and speak with the attorney, make sure you feel good about this person. Bankruptcy is stressful enough without being around someone who makes you feel uncomfortable. I spent some time with different lawyers, before choosing the one that felt right for me.

There are numerous high-quality Law Offices who will provide legal services to individuals in need of experienced legal counsel and possibly Bankruptcy protection. Their reputations have been built on assisting honest people burdened with overwhelming debt. They assist in obtaining what the United States Federal Bankruptcy Courts refers to as a "fresh start" or what they may call "regaining your financial control".

A competent bankruptcy lawyer provides guidance for clients in working their way from unmanageable debt to regaining financial stability. Your lawyer should have consideration for you as an individual and address your specific needs.

Bankruptcy is a very complex issue. You'll find there are different types of bankruptcies, which produce different results. It's vital to choose the right lawyer, to answer all your questions and represent you in court.

Research and find a lawyer whose primary emphasis is on consumer bankruptcy law. An established law firm should have a mission statement reflecting the firm's commitment to serving the needs of everyday people with everyday issues.

Experienced Bankruptcy Law Firms believe that the more informed a client is with respect to the bankruptcy laws and the entire process, the more comfortable they'll feel.

Having the knowledge of what to expect will help to allow people to regain their financial control. A bankruptcy lawyer should take the time to listen, counsel and help provide the proper legal solution for their clients under federal and state laws.

You owe it to yourself to consider all of your options and find a bankruptcy attorney who will guide you, answer all your questions and help you and your family to find a resolution to your personal financial issues.

Actions to Avoid Before Filing Bankruptcy

Believe it or not, there are some actions that you absolutely need to avoid before you file for bankruptcy. The creditors and bankruptcy court can even consider some of these actions as fraud.

The actions a potential bankruptcy debtor should avoid can be organized into three groups.

The first group includes actions that are forbidden by Bankruptcy Code and may cause your case to be dismissed.

The second group includes transactions that are not forbidden by the Bankruptcy Code but can get you in trouble with the Trustee, and even cause certain debts not to be discharged, or potentially result in having the transaction forcibly reversed.

The last group includes actions that are not necessarily going to cause problems in the bankruptcy process but are certainly unwise.

In order to get the fresh start you desire and to help ensure a successful discharge, the following is a brief, non-comprehensive discussion of the things you should avoid doing prior to filing bankruptcy.

The first major issue is fraud. The most common basis for denying a debtor's bankruptcy discharge is because the debtor either hid assets or fraudulently transferred them prior to filing. Some people will take this action in an effort to keep their assets out of the hands of their creditors. The Bankruptcy code was set up to give relief to honest debtors. Committing fraud is illegal and will be basis for a denial of discharge.

The next issue may not be quite as obvious, but is equally enforceable. This issue is a debtor's conversion of non-exempt assets into an exempt form prior to filing bankruptcy. An example of this would be a person who, the week before filing for bankruptcy, takes all of their cash and puts it into their protected (exempt) retirement account. These types of cases usually revolve around the debtor's intent. When there is no direct evidence of intent, the court can draw its own conclusions by looking at certain factors, such as how soon bankruptcy was filed, after the asset conversion was made.

Other actions that can cause the denial of a debtor's discharge are pre-filing actions that involve the purposeful destruction or hiding of financial records.

The bankruptcy trustee and the Court, in general, require certain documentary evidence of a debtor's financial history in the time leading up to bankruptcy. If those documents are not provided and a sufficient, provable excuse can't be provided as to why, the Court can deny your discharge altogether for failure to maintain records. This tends to be more of an issue when small businesses are involved or assets can't be located, but, in any case, should not be taken lightly.

What Debts Won't be Discharged?

Some debts are not dischargeable due to the unique status granted to them by Congress and the courts. Other debts are not dischargeable because of improper actions taken by a debtor in relation to that particular debt. You'll need to get legal advice on this issue, as laws may vary by state. Just be aware that these actions could cause you some real problems.

These types of actions are all rooted in fraud and generally include:

- **Luxury Good or Services** - Includes consumer debts owed to one creditor for amounts higher than $550 incurred in the 90 days before filing bankruptcy.

- **Cash Advances** - Includes cash advances taken within 70 days before a bankruptcy filing totaling more than $825.
- **False Financial Statements** - For example, if you grossly misstate your income on a car loan application in order ensure approval.
- **Debt Incurred Through Actual Fraud** - For example, if you get a signature loan with no intent to pay it back or write a check which you know will bounce.

Ordinarily, an adversary proceeding must be successfully brought by the creditor alleging these types of fraud in order for that particular debt to be rendered non-dischargeable. While adversary proceedings, in general, are rare, it is best to play it safe and avoid any of the above actions, if you want a smooth bankruptcy.

Another issue, which doesn't involve discharge but can have negative consequences, is the "preference doctrine".

The "preference doctrine" basically states that any payments made to general creditors in the 90 days prior to filing bankruptcy or to "insiders", such as family members, in the year prior to filing bankruptcy, can be considered inequitable payments and undone by the bankruptcy trustee.

The exact requirements for determining a preferential payment are complex and beyond the scope of this book. Basically, what this means is if you decide to pay back a family member in the year prior to filing for bankruptcy and not pay other creditor's debts, the trustee may sue the family member to take the money back, in order to distribute it to all your creditors. So it's really something you want to avoid.

8 Actions to Avoid Before Filing for Bankruptcy

Many people will do these exact things before they actually file. Often times, they're trying to avoid filing for bankruptcy, but because their circumstances are so dire, they end up having to file anyhow and now they've made their financial situation even worse.

When considering filing for bankruptcy, here are 8 things you should NOT do.

1. **DO NOT Run Up Your Credit Cards.**

   When some people decide they're going to file for bankruptcy, they think they can use their credit cards to purchase gifts, take a cruise or buy that new 52" flat screen television they've been wanting. But, if you do this, you may be in for a very unpleasant surprise.

Luxury goods over $550 are not dischargeable, if purchased within 90 days of your filing date. Also, the credit card company is more likely to challenge your discharge, if the debit was incurred shortly before filing.

If the credit card company can convince the court you incurred the charges knowing you were going to file for bankruptcy, it will be considered fraud and the charges will not be dischargeable. In addition, you could also face dismissal of your bankruptcy and other legal penalties for fraud.

2. **DO NOT Take a Cash Advance Against Your Credit Cards**

Similar to charging luxury goods to your credit cards, cash advances taken right before you file will not be dischargeable, and you will remain liable for repaying that debt. The reason for the cash advance will be irrelevant to the trustee.

3. **DO NOT Cash Out Your Retirement Account.**

Many people will use their retirement accounts to try to pay their bills, and then end up filing for bankruptcy anyways, once their savings and retirement are gone.

Retirement accounts are normally protected in bankruptcy, so there is no need to use up those funds. Not only will you have no nest egg for your future, you'll also pay income tax, and possibly penalties, on the amounts withdrawn.

Finally, a retirement account distribution may affect your means test, because the amounts withdrawn will be counted toward your income.

Protect your future by saving your retirement for its intended purpose.

4. **DO NOT Get a Home Equity Loan**.

People facing financial difficulties will often take out a home equity loan to consolidate credit card or other unsecured debt. This is a horrible idea because you are now putting your home at risk.

Unsecured debts can be discharged in bankruptcy, but if you want to keep your house, in most cases, you will have to continue paying the home equity loan.

5. **DO NOT Transfer Property.**

   Now is not the time to transfer assets such as cars, boats, real estate, etc. If you do not receive fair market value for the transfer, it could be considered a fraudulent transfer. The trustee can go after the person who received the property to get either the asset itself or the cash value of that particular asset.

6. **DO NOT Pay Back Money to Friends or Relatives.**

   This is definitely not the time to pay back any money you may have borrowed from family or friends.

   If you make any repayments of debts to family or friends within one year prior to filing your petition for bankruptcy, you must disclose those payments on your petition and to the trustee at your meeting of the creditors.

   The bankruptcy court considers these payment to be preferential, insider payments. In other words, this means you are using money that could have gone to pay your other creditors to pay back people you know.

The court can recover these payments from the person you paid. You wouldn't want your family or friends to receive a letter, or phone call, from the trustee telling them that they now owe money to the court. This could most definitely cause a strain in those relationships.

7. **DO NOT Ignore Your Financial Problems.**

When you're overwhelmed by debt, and under a lot of stress, it is easy to procrastinate and try to ignore the problem. But using this tactic can cause even more stress in your life. You're more likely to end up having your wages garnished or bank account levied, not to mention the constant creditor phone calls.

Most people feel a great sense of relief after filing. This is because they no longer have the crushing financial burden hanging over their head or the constant phone calls from creditors.

So, the earlier you deal with the problem, the faster you'll get relief. And the sooner you'll be able to get on with your life.

8. DO NOT Pay Off One Particular Credit Card

It's not in your best interest to pay off one particular credit card with the hopes of keeping it after the bankruptcy. You may find the payment reclaimed as a preferential payment.

Additionally, the credit card company could even cancel your card due to your lowered credit score once the bankruptcy has been discharged.

5 Things to Do Before Filing Bankruptcy

These 5 steps need to be taken when you've decided that bankruptcy is your only option.

1. **File Your Taxes.**

   It's important that you file your tax return before you file for bankruptcy. When you file for bankruptcy, it is expected that you will have filed all of your tax returns. You'll be required to give your trustee a copy of your most recent tax return.

   If you have not filed your taxes, your bankruptcy can be dismissed. Also, if you expect a tax refund, it is important to know how much you will be receiving so you'll know if you can exempt (protect) the refund.

2. **Quit Paying Unsecured Debts.**

   Most unsecured debts will be discharged in bankruptcy, so you will have no further liability for those. Unsecured debts include things like credit cards, personal loans and lines of credit, and medical debts.

   Once you've decided to file for bankruptcy, it no longer makes sense to pay these debts. You're just throwing money away. Believe me, once you file, it's not going to make any difference that you tried to pay these debts.

   You'll need to continue making payments for the following unsecured debts:

   - Student loans
   - Most past due taxes
   - Child support

   These debts are not normally discharged in a bankruptcy. These debts will need to be paid.

3. **Keep Paying for Items You Want to Keep.**

    If you want to keep your house, car, or any other asset with a loan against it, you must continue making your payments on those debts. Once the bankruptcy is discharged, you'll be given the chance to reaffirm these debts.

    Also, in some cases, you must be current on your house to file for Chapter 7 bankruptcy.

4. **Stop Using Credit Cards.**

    If you knowing incur debt after you know you're going to file for bankruptcy, that debt is not dischargeable. It is also possible that your entire bankruptcy could be dismissed for fraud. Remember, fraud has legal penalties.

5. **Get Your Credit Report.**

    It's important to pull a current copy of your credit report. That way you can see exactly what you owe and to whom. It will help you (and your lawyer) understand your overall financial picture and decide whether bankruptcy is your best option.

    You can get your credit report for all three credit reporting agencies at www.annualcreditreport.com. This site allows you to pull one free report, from each of the three agencies, once per year.

This site does not require a credit card and, unlike many sites you see on TV. However, it does require you to subscribe to a credit monitoring service, which you can cancel at any time.

Be sure to pull all 3 reports because it's common for debts to show on one report but not another.

Also, by pulling all 3 reports, this will give you the chance to correct any errors you may find. Correcting any mistakes is very important. It may take a little time, but it's a necessary step.

Documents Needed in Order to File

There are a lot of documents you and your lawyer will need in order to prepare your bankruptcy petition, many of which require you to go back to previous years in order to pull information.

To be able to file promptly, start pulling information regarding your income, debts, assets, and expenses before visiting the attorney.

Some of the documents you'll need to include:

- **Pay Stubs** – Bring pay stubs for the last 6 months
- **Bank and Investment Statements -** (including investment and retirement accounts) for the past 3 months

- **Tax returns** for the past 2-4 years
- **Vehicle Titles** - you'll need copies of car, motorcycle, boat, trailer and any other vehicle you have titled
- **Recorded Deeds and Mortgage**(s) - for your house and any other real estate you may own.
- **Insurance Policies** – be sure to bring copies of all insurance policies
- **Leases and/or Contracts** - copies of any leases or contracts
- **Divorce judgment** – be sure to bring a copy if you have been divorced within the last 6 years
- **Lawsuits and Garnishments** - copies of any lawsuits and/or garnishments
- **Assets** – Make a list of *ALL* of your assets and estimated values
- **Monthly Expenses** –You'll need a list of your monthly expenses

Find an Attorney. Although by law you are not required to have a lawyer to file for bankruptcy, it is generally a bad idea to do it yourself. Bankruptcy is a highly complicated area of law, which changes frequently. If you do it yourself and don't do it correctly, it will likely end up costing you more to have a lawyer fix it, than it would have to hire one from the start. Make sure that you find a lawyer that is responsive and that makes you feel comfortable.

Meeting of Creditors

Sounds kind of scary, doesn't it? It's really not too bad, if you know what to expect. The following should help you understand what this entails and help to put you a little more at ease.

Every person or business filing for bankruptcy protection will be required to attend a meeting of creditors, which is presided over by the bankruptcy trustee. This meeting is sometimes referred to as the "341" meeting, because it's required under Section 341 of the Bankruptcy Code.

This meeting is scheduled approximately 30 – 45 days after the petition for a chapter 7 bankruptcy filed. Normally it's scheduled about 60 days after a case is filed for a chapter 13.

The meeting of the creditors gives the creditors and trustee their first opportunity to ask questions of the bankruptcy filer. What you may want to know here is that the creditors rarely attend the meeting of creditors.

In most bankruptcy cases, there aren't any issues for creditors to investigate, so they won't waste the time and money to attend or send an attorney to ask questions. However, they will attend if they believe they have grounds to object to the bankruptcy discharge. They may feel they have grounds if the debtor was involved in some sort of fraud or improper conduct prior to filing their petition for bankruptcy protection.

What you can expect to happen in the meeting is that the trustee will call out the case number and name of the bankruptcy filer. Don't let this bother you; the only other people in the room are other bankruptcy filers and their lawyers, so everyone is there for the same reason. Believe me, they aren't going to judge you; they're all too busy worrying about themselves.

The trustee will begin by asking you for valid identification and proof of your social security number. If you don't have a social security number, normally a W-2 or 1099 will be acceptable. If you don't have a Social Security Card, check with the court clerk before the meeting to see what other form of ID will be acceptable.

It's normal to feel anxious before the creditors meeting, but try to relax. The most important thing is to tell the truth. The trustee will question you for about 5 minutes. Most of these questions are answered with a "Yes" or "No".

After the trustee finishes asking you all the necessary questions, they will ask if there are any creditors present. If no one speaks up, the meeting will be concluded. At this point, you and your lawyer will leave.

That's pretty much all there is to it. So go, try to relax, answer the questions and leave. It should be pretty quick and painless, unless, of course, you've committed some type of fraud. That probably won't be very pleasant for you.

Final Thoughts

Remember to first do whatever you can to avoid bankruptcy. Make some calls to try working with your creditors, look at getting on a budget, and/or check out debit consolidation.

Expect it to take some time for your credit score to improve after a bankruptcy discharge. You will run into some problems with higher interest rates and even more difficulty when applying for loans.

Be sure not to make mistakes, before filing, that will complicate or even cause your bankruptcy to be dismissed. Keep your all ducks in a row!

Remember your pre-filing actions can cause major problems and even be considered as fraud, under some circumstances.

Don't kid yourself that it's the "easy way out", it's not. It can be very stressful, not to mention embarrassing, but there will be light at the end of the tunnel. Hang in there, be honest with yourself and with the court, and you'll be fine.

Always do your research. Whether it's credit consolidation or a bankruptcy lawyer, be sure you know exactly who you're planning to do business with. You have enough going on, you don't need any more unpleasant surprises.

Don't be afraid of the process. I came out of my bankruptcy a new person and I'm much better off for it. It was tough, no doubt about it, but if it's the right decision for you, then do it and get on with your life.

This might be quite embarrassing for you, but you need to put that aside for now. Just do it and start over. It will most probably be slow going in the beginning, but things will get better over time.